Reaching for God's Hand

Also by Lisa Aré Wulf

Enfolded in God's Arms
40 Reflections to Embrace Your Inner Healing

On a Quest for Christ
Tracing the Footsteps of Your Spiritual Journey

Silent Moments with God Series

Reaching for God's Hand

40 Reflections to Deepen Your Faith Journey

Lisa Aré Wulf

Spiritual Formation House™
Colorado Springs, Colorado
www.spiritualformationhouse.com

Cover Design by Fresh Vision Design
Interior Design by Wood Nymph Creations
Cover Photograph by Kim (Fotolia)
Author Photograph by Katie Corinne Photography

Publisher's Cataloging-in-Publication Data

Names: Wulf, Lisa Are, 1950-, author.
Title: Reaching for God's hand : 40 reflections to deepen your faith journey / by Lisa Aré Wulf.
Series: Silent Moments with God
Description: Colorado Springs, CO: Spiritual Formation House, 2020.
Identifiers: LCCN: 2020940101 | ISBN 978-1-938042-13-3 (Hardcover) | 978-1-938042-12-6 (pbk.) | 978-1-938042-14-0 (Kindle) | 978-1-938042-15-7 (epub) | 978-1-938042-16-4 (audio)
Subjects: LCSH Christian living. | Devotional exercises. | Devotional calendars. | Bible. Minor Prophets--Devotional literature. | BISAC RELIGION / Christian Living / Devotional
Classification: LCC BV4832.2 .W84 2020 | DDC 242/.3--dc23

Published by Spiritual Formation House™
3154 Vickers Dr.
Colorado Springs, CO 80918
www.spiritualformationhouse.com

Printed in the United States of America

To all who seek God

Contents

The Journey Begins   13

Act Justly

1. Look and See   19

2. Pass It On   23

3. Making Choices   27

4. Telling the Truth   31

5. Don't Wanna Do It   35

6. Those Pesky Logs   39

7. The Little People   43

8. Easy Street   47

9. Turning Point   51

10. Christ's Treasures   55

Love Mercy

11. Walking Home   61

12. Too Loud   65

13. Servers   69

14. Low Point   73

15. Giving or Getting   77

16. It's Free   81

17. Every Day Counts   85

18. My Proof   89

19. What You Don't See   93

20. Where Are You?   97

Walk Humbly

21. Gotta Have It   103

22. Super-Hero   107

23. Laundry Boycott   111

24. Walk Through the Gate 115

25. Road to Simplicity   119

26. A Tiny Speck   123

27. Buying Dishes   127

28. Blah Blah Blah   131

29. Not Forgotten   135

30. Bling   139

With Your God

31. Tricks of the Trade   145

32. By Ear   149

33. Pushing Pause   153

34. Hidden Jewels   157

35. Taking a Risk   161

36. God's Orchestra   165

37. Opportunity Knocks   169

38. In the Meantime   173

39. Taming the Worry Monster   177

40. The Tie That Binds   181

The Journey Continues   185

Acknowledgements

I am delighted to thank these very special friends whose contributions and support for this book have been invaluable:

My fabulous editor, Kim McCauley, whose expertise, patience, and friendship were indispensable to this effort.

My two great test readers, Jan Malvern and Jerusha Goebel, whose insights and encouragement refined and shaped this offering.

My excellent proofreader, Susan Defosset, whose eagle eye carefully combed through every inch of the manuscript.

My wonderful husband, Calvin, for his sage advice, encouragement, and patience through endless readings and conversation.

Thanks to each one. This book has become a reality because of you!

The Journey Begins

What does the LORD require of you?
To act justly and to love mercy
and to walk humbly with your God.
Micah 6:8b (NIV)

Why do we do what we do? Where do our thoughts, reactions, and emotions come from? Most of us rarely stop to consider these mysteries. Always busy, we just live our lives. The more important question, though, relates not so much to what we do, but to who we are inside. Is your way of life, with its many decisions and commitments, consistent with the person you strive to be?

We need a framework—something central to our being—to help with those everyday choices. The Old Testament prophet Micah has a perfect plan, and his message is easy to understand. Treat others fairly, be kind and compassionate, and walk with God in a simple and unpretentious way. That's it—easy, right?

But simple plans still present challenges. In real life, we face gray areas. We are tempted to make unwise choices. Often we don't even realize what we're doing as we operate on autopilot. Yet, if we take the time, we can look deep into our souls through prayer and introspection. Our lives will embrace a fresh sense of purpose as we discover better ways to relate to ourselves, to others, and to God.

Reaching for God's Hand: 40 Reflections to Deepen Your Faith Journey is part of the Silent Moments with God series. Each chapter addresses a key character trait for those seeking the Lord. These meditations are loosely gathered into four categories:

Act Justly
Love Mercy
Walk Humbly
With Your God

Each reflection begins with a Scripture verse, followed by a short devotional and a few questions to ponder. Also included are an excerpt from a Psalm and a brief prayer. As your reflection ends, take a minute to journal the truth of your own life experience.

Don't skip over the special section in each chapter titled, "A Silent Moment with God." It's important to pause during your reflection and sit quietly. Open your mind to hear what Jesus is saying to you.

Of course, these devotionals don't cover all situations. Some respond to similar issues from different points of view.

But they all ask you to think. Do you have blind spots? Does your perspective need a tune-up? Wherever you are on Micah's path, one thing is certain. God will walk with you, holding your hand throughout your journey.

Every day, you stand at a crossroads. Which route will you take? What direction will you pursue? Hold these words of Scripture in your heart as you seek the way of Micah.

> *This is what the Lord says:*
> *"Stand at the crossroads and look;*
> *ask for the ancient paths,*
> *ask where the good way is, and walk in it,*
> *and you will find rest for your souls."*
> *Jeremiah 6:16a (NIV)*

I wish you the best on your journey of self-discovery. May you find justice, mercy, and humility as you walk hand-in-hand with God.

Lisa

Act Justly

❧

Truly seeing someone brings hope
and healing to a struggling soul.

Look and See

Blessed are your eyes because they see,
and your ears because they hear.
Matthew 13:16 (NIV)

"Eyes that look are common; eyes that see are rare."
—J. Oswald Sanders, missionary and author.

We've all had conversations with people who didn't see us for who we were—our inner selves, our spiritual depths. It happens every day. Our companions may be just killing time with a chat until an important appointment. Or perhaps they lack the emotional ability to know others on a deeper level. The most likely reason, however, is that they don't see us because they want us to see *them*.

We're also guilty of not seeing others. We may be too busy or tied up in our own world to gaze into another's heart. Those who need our care and understanding walk sadly away, disconnected and alone.

There is an even larger issue we may fail to see. Inequality and injustice are frequent in our world, yet often hidden from view. Those suffering from discrimination, violence, and poverty long to be seen and their voices heard. Are we afraid to notice—or unwilling to listen?

Instances of injustice are everywhere. We may not encounter them directly in our own lives, but we each have friends and acquaintances who struggle. Many strangers we pass on the street face hardship and frustration.

Responding to others can be a challenge. Circumstances often seem overwhelming and hopeless. Still, truly seeing someone, even for an instant, brings hope and healing to a soul struggling to find the way.

Jesus himself doesn't merely glance at us. He sees profoundly into each soul. Imagine the riveting effect of locking eyes with him. If we're called to be like Jesus, it's time to stop looking and genuinely see.

> *Imitate God, therefore, in everything you do,*
> *because you are his dear children.*
> *Live a life filled with love,*
> *following the example of Christ.*
> *Ephesians 5:1-2a (NLT)*

Be Still

for a

Silent Moment with God

Digging Deeper

Are you not seeing someone? Who and why?

If you could truly understand this person, how would that affect him or her?

What steps could you take with God to see others as they genuinely are?

Prayer for Today

I try hard to look and connect with people, God, but I'm not always successful. Yet I've experienced what it feels like to be "unseen" by someone else. Help me focus on what needs to be seen and heard. Together we can bring healing for many. Amen.

Your Thoughts

❦

What we do today matters.
What we do every day matters.

REFLECTION 2

Pass It On

Since we are surrounded by
such a great cloud of witnesses,
let us throw off everything that hinders
and the sin that so easily entangles.
And let us run with perseverance
the race marked out for us.
Hebrews 12:1 (NIV)

The film *Amistad* tells the story of a slave trial that went before the Supreme Court in 1841. Cinqué, the leader of the African captives, calls up the strength of his forefathers to help him through the trial. He even states, "For at this moment, I am the whole reason they have existed at all."

The scene carries a powerful message. What we do today matters. What we do every day matters.

We are now carrying the torch of faith—the same beacon believers have carried for 2000 years. In holding the lantern high, we bring Christianity to new generations. If we let the flame sputter and die, those who follow won't receive the gift.

Today we stand on the stage of history. The actions and prayers of Christ's followers through the centuries have paved the way to our place on that stage. Who we are reflects their faithfulness. In a sense, Cinqué was right. From his perspective, the earliest Christians existed for the sake of today.

Our spiritual ancestors, the cloud of witnesses, are watching us run our race. We can tap into the fortitude and commitment they offer. They encourage each runner in the marathon and cheer when we enter the stadium.

So, what will we do with that torch of faith? Let's run the race with all our strength. Rather than wander off the track, let's pass on the faith our forebears preserved. God, our biggest fan, is running right alongside us.

I have fought the good fight,
I have finished the race,
I have kept the faith.
2 Timothy 4:7 (NIV)

Be Still
for a
Silent Moment with God

Digging Deeper

How have you benefitted from the devotion of earlier believers?

What are you doing now to preserve and pass along the faith?

Where is God in your plans?

Prayer for Today

When I remember those who came before me, God, I am in awe of their devotion and steadfastness. Help me carry on the faith they tenderly nurtured for me. At this moment, I'm the reason they persevered. Walk with me as I honor the hope that ennobled their lives. Amen.

Your Thoughts

❦

God longs for each of us to become
beacons of light and compassion.

REFLECTION 3

Making Choices

*But the wisdom that comes from heaven
is first of all pure;
then peace-loving, considerate, submissive,
full of mercy and good fruit,
impartial and sincere.*
James 3:17 (NIV)

Every day brings new choices. Some days our decisions may be good; other days, not so much.

Many choices involve how we treat others. Are we inflexible and judgmental, never extending grace unless it's to our benefit? Or are we compassionate, filled with love and forgiveness for them and ourselves?

The people who come into our orbit are a precious trust, deserving of our consideration. If we listen to them, respect who they are, and love them through good times and bad, we send a message of hope and encouragement. They, in turn, feel cherished and supported.

Another daily choice we face involves living with integrity. Have we carefully considered our values and whether our actions reflect them? Are we truthful about our abilities—what we can and can't do? Honesty in our lives, even if reflected imperfectly, may inspire many to do the same.

The most important choice we face every day is about God. Some make a conscious decision to turn away from him. With each step, they walk further and further along the path of separation. The better and equally deliberate choice is to run in his direction, growing ever closer to him. God is always waiting nearby, longing to stroll hand-in-hand with us throughout our lives.

And what about God's choices? Because his nature is love, he has only one—to forgive and welcome each person back who returns to him, no matter what. He longs for each of us to become beacons of light and compassion.

You hold daily decisions in your own hands. Which way are you turning?

Those who say they live in God
should live their lives as Jesus did.
1 John 2:6 (NLT)

Be Still
for a
Silent Moment with God

Digging Deeper

What are your most difficult choices? Why are they challenging?

In what ways could you change how you approach them?

How do you sense God leading you in your decision-making process?

Prayer for Today

Sometimes my choices aren't the best. It's such a struggle. Help me, God. Lead me as I seek a life of love and integrity—the life you want for me. Be with me as together we walk the path set out for me. Amen.

Your Thoughts

❧

We can open the door
to God's healing grace.

Telling the Truth

For we are taking pains to do what is right,
not only in the eyes of the Lord
but also in the eyes of man.
2 Corinthians 8:21 (NIV)

Sometimes the truth hurts. Most of us are compassionate people who don't wish to cause distress. We're tempted to sugar-coat, tell little white lies, or just ignore awkward dilemmas altogether. But in crucial situations, telling the truth is the best option.

Let's consider a story about two gravely ill newborn babies. Both died shortly after birth. In the first case, the doctors wanted to spare the parents' feelings, so they didn't share that the baby would not survive the next few hours. When the infant suddenly passed away, the couple was shocked and devastated.

The other physicians were truthful with the second parents about their baby's condition. This couple took their child outside for a short time to feel the warm sun, touch the cool grass, and taste ice cream. Afterward, the mother was glad she knew the truth so her son could have these experiences before he died.

Which physicians were more helpful? The first doctors tried to shield the family by skirting the truth. These parents didn't expect their baby to die. Being prepared may have softened the loss and eased their sorrow.

The second doctors gave the parents a choice. It was still a hard situation. But after getting over the initial shock, this family was able to build memories with their newborn.

What's the lesson? Sometimes we just need to tell the truth—no matter how difficult. By doing so, we enable others to make reasonable decisions. Instead of clinging to false hope, we open the door to God's healing grace.

We will speak the truth in love,
growing in every way more and more like Christ,
who is the head of his body, the church.
Ephesians 4:15 (NLT)

Be Still
for a
Silent Moment with God

Digging Deeper

Describe a time you struggled to tell the truth.

Do you wish you had handled the scenario differently? How?

How could God strengthen and guide you in similar situations?

Prayer for Today

I really don't like to hurt people, God. It may be okay to spare their feelings in minor things, but sometimes it's best to just be honest. Help me to know the difference. Together we can be a tender and compassionate presence for those who need to face a hard truth. Amen.

Your Thoughts

❧

Our best choice is always trusting God
to tell us what to do.

Don't Wanna Do It

In their hearts humans plan their course,
but the LORD establishes their steps.
Proverbs 16:9 (NIV)

We've all been there. Someone asks us to do something. Maybe they pressure us to take part in a project. We feel guilty and say yes. Then we regret it. Perhaps we lack the time or interest. Or we have no idea why it bothers us. All we know is that we just don't want to do it.

Is there a value in doing tasks we'd rather not do? Spiritual disciplines help us grow in our faith and relationship with God. Some activities, like prayer or eating vegetables, have a clear benefit. Others are not so obvious. Must we take part? Can we simply opt out?

Once I committed to a volunteer job I did not look forward to at all. The project was worthwhile. Plus, I was well qualified. But the closer it got, the more I sensed resentment creeping into my thoughts.

The world tells us to do what we enjoy and forget the rest. But what about serving Christ? If I'm able to do something, can I choose not to do it? Can I turn down such requests and concentrate on what I prefer to do?

This is a thorny question. Jesus doesn't make our lives miserable by calling us into areas where we aren't gifted. But just being qualified for a task shouldn't always mean we must do it either.

When we face these situations, let's talk with Jesus about our motivations and fears. Maybe our concerns are justified, and the activity would waste valuable time. Or perhaps he has someone else in mind for the task. How can we tell?

Our best choice is always trusting God to tell us what to do. Listen closely, and he will whisper the answer.

Work willingly at whatever you do,
as though you were working for the Lord
rather than for people.
Colossians 3:23 (NLT)

Be Still
for a
Silent Moment with God

Digging Deeper

Describe a time you agreed to a task you didn't want to do.

Did you sense God leading you? How did it turn out?

Were you happy or disappointed with the outcome? Why?

Prayer for Today

I have endless invitations to activities I'd rather not join. Am I just too popular? Seriously, I need your guidance, God. Help me sort out the requests. Show me which to accept and the grace to sometimes say no. Lead me along your path. Amen.

Your Thoughts

We often don't perceive ourselves
for who we actually are.

Those Pesky Logs

How can you say to your brother,
"Let me take the speck out of your eye,"
when all the time there is a plank in your own eye?
Matthew 7:4 (NIV)

It's so easy to spot other people's faults. Their defects are obvious, even to a casual observer. But that's not the case with our own faults. We're often perfect in our own eyes— or at least reasonably okay. Why the difference?

Our family and friends are great, and we adore them. We accept that everybody has difficulties, and our loved ones are no exception. We overlook annoying tendencies, peculiar behavior, and irritating words. These blemishes are visible, but we make allowance for them. After all, these are our special people.

Conversely, we are often clueless about our own issues. We find nothing wrong with us, no annoying habits, no idiosyncrasies. We are fine just the way we are, thank you very much! But our personality quirks are glaringly familiar to those we love. And they ignore them, because they love us.

Why are we blind to our own flaws? Perhaps we're convinced of the rightness of our conduct because of our upbringing. Or we may judge ourselves to be inferior, being unable to grasp our own goodness and strengths. Either way, we don't perceive ourselves for who we are.

God asks us to take the log out of our own eyes so we can see the speck in someone else's. Is it time to ask Jesus for the same discernment concerning ourselves that we so easily have about everyone else? Look, he's nodding his head. Yes, it is!

Search me, O God, and know my heart;
test me and know my anxious thoughts.
See if there is any offensive way in me,
and lead me in the way everlasting.
Psalm 139:23-24 (NIV)

Be Still
for a
Silent Moment with God

Digging Deeper

How do you think others see you? Does it match your perception?

In what ways could you view yourself more accurately?

How do you suppose God looks at you?

Prayer for Today

It's so hard to see myself as I truly am. I have no trouble identifying everyone else's faults, but what about mine? Help me, God, to know what's good about me and what isn't. Give me clear vision and the ability to recognize myself through your eyes of love. Amen.

Your Thoughts

৯

Even a small act
can make a difference.

The Little People

*He gives power to the weak
and strength to the powerless.*
Isaiah 40:29 (NLT)

Do you yearn to be famous? Perhaps you hope to be a leader in your field, make a groundbreaking medical discovery, or write an opera. Seeing your name in the news, finding yourself mentioned online, or appearing in a textbook is a cool thought. But is fame a realistic goal? Will history actually remember us? Probably not.

Folks everywhere clamor to be heard. With so many people generating so much noise, it's hard to stand out. But even if we're lost in the crowd, our contributions can be just as significant as anyone else's.

History is a long continuum. First the pendulum swings in one direction, then in another. Through the ages, millions of "little people" have shaped its movement. When enough souls travel together on a particular course, they can set great events in motion. They often affect more change than the superstars.

Consider your voice and experience as a person of faith. Your first assignment is simply to show up. Then choose the issues you're passionate about and enter the conversation. There's no need for a big splash. Just live your best life, knowing that even a tiny act can make a difference.

How we live influences the major controversies of our era. Our contribution, however small, matters. The trajectory of the world may move at a glacial pace, but what we do affects the future.

Whether or not we're written up in a history book, our lives count. Our reflection of God's grace can shape his creation. As more and more of us join the dialogue through words and actions, the arc of the universe shifts. That's a big impact!

Always work enthusiastically for the Lord,
for you know that nothing you
do for the Lord is ever useless.
1 Corinthians 15:58b (NLT)

Be Still
for a
Silent Moment with God

Digging Deeper

What topics are you passionate about? Describe them.

In what ways can you join the dialogue, even on a small scale?

How is God showing you that your voice counts?

Prayer for Today

The history books may never remember me, God, and yet my voice matters. Through quiet, patient words and deeds, I will be heard. Your world is full of significant issues, worthy of debate. Give me confidence to enter the discussion. Walk with me as we influence your creation for the good of everyone. Amen.

Your Thoughts

෨

Recognizing Christ in those around us
requires effort and risk.

REFLECTION 8

Easy Street

Love each other with genuine affection,
and take delight in honoring each other.
Romans 12:10 (NLT)

The conference speaker made a startling statement: "You
see it every day—people climbing over others to get to
Easy Street. They'll do whatever it takes. But living a life of
love is harder. The threat of harm, emotional, physical or
economic, is always there. Kind of like crucifixion."

The room fell silent, pondering his words.

Yes, it's tempting to be shrewd and do anything necessary to win. Our culture admires those who fight their way
to the top. We don't notice when they brush aside someone
who blocks their ladder, stepping over them or pushing them
to the bottom.

Most of us are not vicious. We're just cruising along,
trying to build a productive, flourishing life. Aggressively

harming people isn't in our playbook. But going out of our way to treat them with fairness is another story.

The speaker suggested that a life of love may be rocky. Recognizing Christ in those around us requires effort and risk. Perceiving them as God's children is a daily challenge. While we hope for positive rewards, sometimes we are left with only pain.

Every day we face a choice. Giving up Easy Street to be a person of love can involve a major U-turn. Our emphasis changes from getting ahead to finding God's image in everyone around us.

The way of love is challenging. The reward is a life well lived. Remember Jesus. His legacy is one of tender affection and caring for all of us. In light of his example, how could we do less?

Dear friends,
let us continue to love one another,
for love comes from God.
Anyone who loves is a child of God
and knows God.
1 John 4:7 (NLT)

Be Still
for a
Silent Moment with God

Digging Deeper

What is your definition of success?

Describe your most challenging obstacle to living a life of love.

How might you see others through God's eyes?

Prayer for Today

There is much injustice in the world. Often it's committed by those trying to get ahead on the road to victory and accomplishment. I don't want to use people as stepping-stones to my fulfillment, God. Help me see them as you do—with loving eyes. This path may be full of difficulties, but together we can handle them. Amen.

Your Thoughts

⍦

Perhaps it's time to challenge a
long-held viewpoint.

Turning Point

Trust in the LORD with all your heart;
do not depend on your own understanding.
Proverbs 3:5 (NLT)

Do you have strong opinions? Are you convinced that nothing could ever change your mind? Whether long-held ideas, or a recently formed point of view, most of us believe our thoughts will never be altered. We just can't see any other reasonable position.

But then your world abruptly changes. New insights appear as you encounter an unfamiliar reality. As you approach the situation with fresh eyes, your mind is transformed.

A good friend shared her struggle with me. She grew up in a home with deep-seated notions about certain types of people. They were considered undesirable and definitely not trustworthy. Her family's advice was clear: avoid those folks at all costs.

Years later, when she met one of "those folks," her former convictions were shattered. He was a regular guy with genuine struggles and triumphs. She listened to his story, the tale of a life unlike hers, yet remarkably similar. As she peered into his soul, her previously unquestioned beliefs changed in an instant.

We typically don't realize our old programming can be a problem. We carry long-established beliefs, often passed down through our families. Why would we do anything differently or even examine our mindset?

God asks that we be fair and just. Perhaps it's time to challenge a long-held viewpoint and be willing to adjust our thinking and actions. We may emerge with a brand-new outlook.

Think about how Jesus works. He allows us to follow a chosen path, carrying attitudes gathered throughout our lives. Then one day, a new and vivid reality appears and his perspective shines up ahead. When that happens, will we open our eyes? Will we see as he sees? What will change? Maybe everything!

Don't copy the behavior and customs of this world,
but let God transform you into a new person
by changing the way you think.
Romans 12:2a (NLT)

Be Still
for a
Silent Moment with God

Digging Deeper

Who or what do you perceive differently today? Explain the shift.

In what ways could you act on this change?

How might God lead you to a truer understanding?

Prayer for Today

I know I don't always observe people correctly. Sometimes I'm downright judgmental. Help me, God, to experience others as they truly are. Give me a heart to understand their stories, their struggles, and their joys. I want to see as Jesus sees—with eyes full of love. Amen.

Your Thoughts

∽

Justice requires that we treat our neighbors
with fairness and respect.

Christ's Treasures

Those who oppress the poor insult their Maker,
but helping the poor honors him.
Proverbs 14:31 (NLT)

Laurence served as a deacon in the early church in Rome. During a season of Christian persecution, the Roman authorities demanded information about the wealth of his congregation. They thought the small band of believers was secretly rich.

So Laurence brought together the poor and sick of his city and presented them to the rulers, saying, "These are the treasures of the church." Not impressed, the Romans roasted him alive in the year 258.

Are the poor and the sick still our treasures? Sometimes they are. But too often they are forgotten, blamed for their troubles, and cast aside as unworthy. Some struggle to find housing, food, and medical care. Many never catch up, no matter how hard they try. They feel left behind, lost, and abandoned.

Why are the poor so often overlooked? Our culture may be partly to blame. The American narrative values rugged individualism. The world tells those who struggle to "pull themselves up by their bootstraps." But what if they have no boots?

Perhaps we've become too self-focused. Getting ahead in today's environment can be tough, and we need every ounce of energy to look after our own interests. Or do we?

Stories of those facing poverty and illness fill the pages of Scripture. Jesus loved them. Laurence died for them. Justice requires that we treat our neighbors with fairness and respect. That means seeing them as children of God, just like us.

The first Christians lived out the gospel, even in martyrdom. Is it time to see the less fortunate with ancient eyes— the way Jesus sees them?

If anyone has material possessions
and sees a brother or sister in need
but has no pity on them,
how can the love of God be in that person?
1 John 3:17 (NIV)

Be Still
for a
Silent Moment with God

Digging Deeper

Is helping the poor and sick part of your life? How?

How could you balance your interests with those who are struggling?

In what ways might God lead you to creative new insights on caring for others?

Prayer for Today

I'm guilty as charged! I know others struggle, often through no fault of their own, God. But sometimes I am so busy just trying to get by that I give them no thought. Help me be compassionate and generous with my own resources, however meager they may be. Amen.

Your Thoughts

Love Mercy

ॐ

Our hearts long to journey
with our loved ones.

Walking Home

Love never gives up, never loses faith,
is always hopeful,
and endures through every circumstance.
1 Corinthians 13:7 (NLT)

The photo was striking. Two older ladies walked together in a rainstorm. One held an umbrella, shielding their heads from the rain. The caption said, "We're all just walking each other home."

This lovely sentiment captures the essence of Christian community. Side-by-side, we walk toward our final home of rest with Jesus. During this journey, we are called to support each other, bear with one another's faults, grieve as one in moments of sorrow, and share in times of joy. Whatever the challenge, we're in this together.

It sounds nice, but reality isn't always so easy. Life gets in the way and shatters the perfect picture. Some people aren't as considerate as we hope they'd be. Sometimes we're not very kind either. Our hopes go awry for many reasons. What can we do?

No matter how much we wish to stroll all the way home with those closest to us, this isn't always possible. Rifts occur that cannot be mended, regardless of how hard we try. Or our loved ones may be thousands of miles away, making travel impossible. But our hearts still long to journey with them.

Perhaps the solution is spiritual, rather than literal. One way to be with our loved ones is through prayer. Why not lay that troubled relationship on the altar and continue the trek on a divine plane?

Let's not forget that each of us is also walking home with God. Our time on earth is short, and we couldn't ask for a better travel companion than Jesus. How delightful to hold his hand and gaze at the scenery as we amble toward eternity together.

If it is possible, as far as it depends on you,
live at peace with everyone.
Romans 12:18 (NIV)

Be Still
for a
Silent Moment with God

Digging Deeper

Are you walking home with someone, or do you hope to? How?

If loved ones are missing from your life, in what ways could you still walk with them?

How do you see yourself walking home with Jesus?

Prayer for Today

Whether going home after a rainstorm or stepping toward eternity, I love the thought of walking together. But it isn't always easy. Help me, God, to travel with those who are willing. Keep me in spirit with those who are absent. And let me stroll with you forever into paradise. Amen.

Your Thoughts

୶

Seek to uplift each other
so all are understood and respected.

Too Loud

Anyone with ears to hear should listen
and understand!
Matthew 11:15 (NLT)

It was the regular Thursday night choir practice. As the volume got louder and louder, a few voices dominated, while the rest of the group seemed muffled. The director clapped his hands to pause the rehearsal. "If you can't hear the person next to you," he said, "you're too loud." What great advice—and not just for singers.

We've all had conversations with folks who talk non-stop about themselves. Scarcely drawing a breath, they relate every event in their lives in excruciating detail. On and on they drone, never stopping to listen. But others have unique stories that deserve attention too. People feel devalued when they are drowned out. Their important perspectives are lost.

Constant talking can be a problem in our Christian world. Are we called to broadcast how magnificent we are? Must we reveal everything about ourselves and our spiritual lives? No, not really. That habit doesn't serve any of the people around us, much less God.

Perhaps the silent person in the group is facing tragic circumstances and needs a sympathetic ear. Compassionate understanding and support might offer hope for the future. Or consider the humble man who rarely speaks. His depth of character may well inspire all who listen. So maybe it's time to give others a chance to express themselves.

True Christian relationship honors everyone, including ourselves. Soul-healing conversations are like a tennis game—back and forth and back and forth. Each side holds the ball for a bit before quickly returning it over the net. Both sides are attentive and seek to uplift each other. Everyone is understood and respected.

Let's tone down the loud singing, tap the ball over the net, and listen.

May the words of my mouth
and the meditation of my heart
be pleasing to you,
O Lord, my rock and my redeemer.
Psalm 19:14 (NLT)

Be Still
for a
Silent Moment with God

Digging Deeper

Describe occasions when you dominated conversations.

What is preventing you from quietly listening to someone else?

Where do you see God's encouragement to stop talking and listen?

Prayer for Today

Talking is so much fun. I love to share everything so that people will know who I am. But that's not fair. Others want to speak too. Sometimes I need to put the brakes on my mouth. With your help, God, I can be a compassionate and caring listener. Amen.

Your Thoughts

≈

If Jesus cares for those in difficult
circumstances, how can we do less?

REFLECTION 13

Servers

A generous person will prosper;
whoever refreshes others will be refreshed.
Proverbs 11:25 (NIV)

A wise pastor challenged his congregation, "I don't care how loudly you sing this morning, how high you raise your arms, or how vigorously you say 'Amen!' during my sermon. None are proof of your Christian commitment. The best sign is how you treat your server at lunch once you leave here."

It's a familiar routine. We walk out of the church, still basking in the love of Jesus, and head over to a pleasant meal. We may wave to friends at the next table or catch the headlines on an overhead TV. But how often do we see— really see—those who serve our food?

Do we greet servers with a friendly smile and maybe call them by name? Do we ask how they're doing? Do we look at them and speak kindly as we place our order?

Sadly, customers are often rude and disdainful. Servers are routinely treated like furniture in the restaurant, as objects that don't matter. But they are valuable souls, whose lives may be full of struggles we can only imagine.

My husband and I have an informal ministry to servers at our favorite restaurants. We know many of their names and listen as they tell their stories. The shy ones always get a wave and a smile. We've occasionally slipped our server friends a bit of money when they were in need.

As Christians, it's easy to be self-absorbed and concerned only with our own religious experience. But Jesus says that when we reach out to help a struggling person, we're reaching out to him too. If he takes time to care for those in difficult circumstances, how can we do less?

> *The King will reply, "Truly I tell you, whatever you did for one of the least of these brothers and sisters of mine, you did for me." Matthew 25:40 (NIV)*

Be Still
for a
Silent Moment with God

Digging Deeper

When you eat out, how do you treat your servers?

What could you do to encourage and build them up?

In what ways can you see Jesus in each one?

Prayer for Today

I confess, God, that I'm not always kind and polite to those who are serving me in stores or restaurants. Help me remember that they are people of value with their own struggles, challenges, and joys. I want to see Jesus in them as I offer encouragement and praise. Amen.

Your Thoughts

༄

With compassion we can lift and restore
a loved one who has disappointed us.

Low Point

This is my commandment:
Love each other in the same way I have loved you.
John 15:12 (NLT)

It's easy to cherish family and friends when everything is going great. Their lives cruise along, no problems in sight, and the horizon is sunny. We walk with them, mix in a bit of encouragement, and celebrate their victories.

But what about when there are no victories? Suppose a friend is struggling and can't get her life together. Hopefully, you can continue to love and support her, maintaining a solid relationship. But what if your friend's struggle negatively impacts you?

In the film *A Raisin in the Sun*, a woman entrusts her life savings to her son. Though he has good intentions, he loses it all through a series of poor decisions, devastating his mother.

He's equally crushed and doesn't believe he deserves her love anymore. Yet his mother knows he was at a low moment. She forgives him, and they move ahead together as a family.

What would you do in this situation? Would you still care for the son, or would you walk away from the relationship? Would you be tempted to get angry, to tell him how upset you are? The money mattered, and now you're left with nothing.

How does Jesus see this situation? Over and over, he asks that we forgive. Of course, we need to keep ourselves safe, physically and emotionally. We needn't expose ourselves over and over to harm. But with God's help, we may be able to compassionately lift and restore a loved one who has disappointed us.

A real test of the Christian life is to hold others close, especially at their worst moments. It's challenging to show faith in a person who has struggled and failed. But our acceptance and encouragement, however difficult, may help to bring someone back from their lowest point.

The LORD is merciful and compassionate,
slow to get angry and filled with unfailing love.
Psalm 145:8 (NLT)

Be Still
for a
Silent Moment with God

Digging Deeper

Describe a situation in which a friend or family member badly hurt you.

How was he or she affected by the circumstances?

Do you sense God leading you to a resolution? How?

Prayer for Today

Other people can be downright difficult. Sometimes they don't seem to care. But there also are those who are genuinely sorry and regret their actions. Help me, God, to find compassion and forgiveness to love them just as you do. Amen.

Your Thoughts

❧

Could God be seeking a partner—
someone like you?

Giving or Getting

*Each of you should use whatever gift
you have received to serve others,
as faithful stewards of God's grace
in its various forms.*
1 Peter 4:10 (NIV)

"Who's here this morning to get something?" the pastor asked as he strode out to begin his sermon. Lots of hands went up. Then he inquired, "How many came here today to give?" A few sheepishly raised their arms.

We all want God's blessing and the abundance he offers. Every day, we ask his help with our needs and struggles. But something's missing. What about giving—not just money, but ourselves?

Centuries ago, a Christian named Teresa of Avila said, "Christ has no body now on earth but yours, no hands, no feet but yours. Yours are the eyes through which he looks with compassion on the world. Yours are the feet with which he is to go about doing good. Yours are the hands with which he is to bless us now."

One of my favorite icons of Jesus is called "The Bread of Life." It depicts Christ rising out of a communion cup. As I seek to reflect this noble concept in my heart, I imagine myself figuratively serving communion to each person I meet. Sometimes I fail to serve as I should, but it helps me focus on being a sacrament to others.

Consider your own life. It's great to receive, but what are you giving? You may think you don't have time or anything to offer. Perhaps the easier option is simply to look away from those in need.

But God has a different plan. Could he be seeking a partner—someone like you? Why not try walking hand-in-hand with him, showing his love to the world? Giving of ourselves can reflect Christ to a hurting humanity that desperately needs his grace.

And do not forget to do good
and to share with others,
for with such sacrifices God is pleased.
Hebrews 13:16 (NIV)

Be Still
for a
Silent Moment with God

Digging Deeper

On the spectrum between getting and giving, where do you see yourself?

How could you move closer to the giving side?

Jesus asks you to be his representative in the world. How can you reflect his love today?

Prayer for Today

Sometimes I go to church just to be "fed." Yes, I'm guilty! But we can accomplish much together, God. Let me be your hands and feet wherever I venture. Teach me how to show your love and grace to all I meet. Amen.

Your Thoughts

꙲

Even the smallest act of kindness
can lift a spirit that's dragging.

It's Free

Anxiety weighs down the heart,
but a kind word cheers it up.
Proverbs 12:25 (NIV)

Do you want your life to matter? Do you hope to leave a legacy of good? Most of us would answer, "yes." It sounds great, but how does one accomplish such a noble mission?

Perhaps you're aware of pressing problems in your community and you'd like to help. You may be passionate about current issues and want to get involved. But do you feel blocked by lack of time, financial worries, or too many other commitments?

Think again. There *is* something you can do. Why not start with simple encouragement? It costs nothing and only takes a minute, but it may soothe a hurting soul. It doesn't require special circumstances or a grand gesture. Even the smallest act of kindness can lift a spirit that's dragging.

Have you ever been helped by a sales clerk who was flustered and made mistakes while scanning your order? Perhaps she admits it's her first day on the job. Letting her know she's doing good work can brighten an otherwise difficult time.

Or have you stood in line and watched the customer ahead of you treat a fast-food server badly? As her eyes fill with pain, a friendly look and kind words help ease the hurt.

We can sympathize, because we've been in these kinds of situations ourselves. Sometimes the day just isn't going well, and troubles multiply. Then a cheerful face smiles and seems to understand our sadness. For that brief second, the burden eases. Our lives feel important.

A friend of mine strives to be a blessing to everyone he meets. Through his encouragement, each new acquaintance is honored and respected, regardless of circumstances. Many can see Christ reflected in his kindness.

So, are you ready to scatter encouragement wherever you go? It's free—and I bet God will smile too.

Kind words are like honey—
sweet to the soul and healthy for the body.
Proverbs 16:24 (NLT)

Be Still
for a
Silent Moment with God

Digging Deeper

Do you see others who struggle but are ignored? Describe them.

How can you be an encouraging presence for them today?

Could you partner with God in this endeavor? How?

Prayer for Today

Open my eyes, God. Every day, I pass by folks with problems. All they want is a glimpse of encouragement, a tiny gesture of respect. Help me to reflect your love and compassion. Let's walk together, bringing hope to a hurting world. Amen.

Your Thoughts

❦

Could our real mission be to
reflect God to those around us?

Every Day Counts

What is your life?
You are a mist that appears
for a little while and then vanishes.
James 4:14b (NIV)

Some days seem to go wrong before they even begin. Perhaps something unpleasant happens, or troubling news comes your way. Sometimes you may wake up with a foggy mind. Whatever the cause, you just want to forget about today and start over again tomorrow.

This is a bad idea—and a misuse of time. I've heard that when we reach a certain age, we can calculate the rest of our lives in months. I'm now at that time of life, and maybe you are too. Do we really want to squander a fraction of a month for each day we throw away? With the end looming in sight, there are no hours to lose!

More importantly, when we give up on a day, our purpose can be wasted. Why are we here on earth—to have fun? Make lots of money? Be famous and admired? That all sounds cool, but those things don't have lasting impact or bring true joy. Could our real mission be to reflect God to those around us? If we take a day off, he isn't any less radiant. But others may not see him as clearly without us.

Our daily walk with God is not always about activity and getting things done. It can be to reveal him to folks when we lend a hand or listen to someone in need. Other times, we rest in his presence to refresh and regroup. All of these choices are pleasing to him.

God longs to spend each day with you and transform it into something beautiful. Stay engaged and make every hour count. Jesus can't wait to share it with you.

Lord, remind me how brief
my time on earth will be.
Remind me that my days are numbered—
how fleeting my life is.
Psalm 39:4 (NLT)

Be Still
for a
Silent Moment with God

Digging Deeper

Are you ever tempted to skip today and try again tomorrow?

In what ways could you make each day count?

How can you reflect God to others in your daily world?

Prayer for Today

When life goes wrong, I just want to crawl back under the covers and forget about today. But I know you have other plans for me, God. Help me live the purpose that you planned for me. Walk with me as I show your love and grace to everyone I meet. Amen.

Your Thoughts

૭

God values each of his children
regardless of their achievements.

My Proof

When God our Savior revealed his
kindness and love, he saved us,
not because of the righteous things we had done,
but because of his mercy.
Titus 3:4-5a (NLT)

We want our lives to matter. We yearn to make a difference. Each of us longs to know we've done a good job. But sometimes we need to offer ourselves a little mercy along the way.

Years ago, I co-hosted a weekly live radio talk program. We featured interesting guests and explored lots of helpful topics. It was so much fun. After each episode, the station announcer handed me a cassette recording that I kept in a box in the garage. (Yes, they really used cassettes—a dead giveaway about how long ago the show aired!)

Cleaning my garage decades later, I found the tapes and pondered what to do. I could digitize them, but doubted that I'd listen to them again. Maybe I should just throw them away. A small voice inside insisted that if I didn't keep them, it would somehow diminish my value as a person. Perhaps I needed the cassettes as evidence to substantiate my accomplishments.

What was I thinking—that I would hand Jesus a bunch of tapes after I die to prove my worth? On some level, I wanted to earn his approval. Finally, though, I realized my broadcasting benefit was not in those recordings. Rather, it lived on in those I had helped. I ended up tossing the box, keeping only a few cassettes as souvenirs. It was the right choice.

God values each of his children, regardless of their achievements. But the exercise in the garage showed me that I still need to learn to accept God's love and mercy. What might you be holding onto as "proof" of your worth?

Give thanks to the LORD, for he is good!
His faithful love endures forever.
1 Chronicles 16:34 (NLT)

Be Still
for a
Silent Moment with God

Digging Deeper

When have you struggled with the need to prove your worth?

Consider how you might view that scene differently.

In what ways does God show you his love, regardless of your accomplishments?

Prayer for Today

I'm struggling, God, and have been for years. Ever since I can remember, I've tried to earn your acceptance through achievement. Help me see my life through your eyes. Cast away my pall of unworthiness as I step into the radiance of your love. Amen.

Your Thoughts

℘

Let us find the courage to
restore the broken pieces of our world.

What You Don't See

Ears to hear and eyes to see—
both are gifts from the LORD.
Proverbs 20:12 (NLT)

Are you an observant person? Do you pay attention to the details of your surroundings? I think we all pride ourselves on knowing and understanding our little piece of the universe. But significant matters may hide from us in plain sight.

A friend mentioned to me that as a child, she often visited the southeastern United States and remembered water fountains marked for "colored folk only." She looked right past them, never stopping to consider what they signified to both black and white people. The fountains simply "were."

What is the impact of not seeing? Those fountains reflected an injustice against a large segment of society. But issues closer to home can routinely elude us too. For example, when wheelchair-bound folks must ride in the street because the curb has no ramp, their safety is compromised. Do we notice and try to help them? Or is this merely how things are?

It's tragic when suffering people don't merit our attention. We avoid the elderly man struggling to cross the intersection. We ignore the woman counting pennies at the fast-food counter to see if she can afford a burger. We steer clear of teens on the street with nowhere to go.

You and I can't heal everyone who suffers, but let's at least recognize them. As we become mindful of their plight, change slowly begins, and souls mend.

Remember all those stories about Jesus healing the blind and restoring their sight? With him as our guide, we now understand what had been veiled. By placing our trust in him, we can find the courage to bring the hidden to light and restore the broken pieces of our world.

Once more Jesus put his hands on the man's eyes.
Then his eyes were opened, his sight was restored,
and he saw everything clearly.
Mark 8:25 (NIV)

Be Still
for a
Silent Moment with God

Digging Deeper

Look around you. What aren't you seeing? Why do you not see it?

How has this "blindness" affected you and others?

In what ways might God help you see better?

Prayer for Today

I always thought I was a sharp-eyed person. Looking back over my life, though, I've missed a lot. There have been struggling people I hardly noticed and hurtful conditions that barely registered. Open my eyes, God, to see what's happening. When we know the truth, change is possible. Amen.

Your Thoughts

❧

Real connections are built on depth,
not distractions.

Where Are You?

Let your eyes look straight ahead;
fix your gaze directly before you.
Give careful thought to the paths for your feet
and be steadfast in all your ways.
Proverbs 4:25-27 (NIV)

Bam! Her racket slams the tennis ball, hurling it across the court and back again, over and over. Wow! She's really focused on her game. But wait—look at her other hand. She's also juggling a cell phone, never dropping a sentence as she chats with a friend.

Sound familiar? We appear to be present, going about our daily business, but our attention can be miles away. We check the news on our phones while buying vegetables at the market. Our boss thinks we're working hard in our cubicle while an entertaining video runs in a tiny window on our computer screen. The media-driven environment allows us to be everywhere, all at the same time. So, where are we exactly?

In today's lifestyle, multi-tasking is expected, if not required. In a culture that encourages distraction, it's tough to be present—even with ourselves. Standing still can be a scary proposition. But unless we do, we may not grow much, personally or spiritually.

Real connections are built on depth, not distractions. It doesn't matter whether we're alone, with others, or with God. We need time to interact, talk, laugh, and cry. Probing the depths of our souls takes courage. But without it, relationships skate on the surface, rather than offering life-giving sustenance.

In these days when everyone seems to be somewhere else, remember that you aren't alone. Someone special is always present and focused on you. Capture this moment—just you and God—together again.

My heart has heard you say, "Come and talk with me."
And my heart responds, "Lord, I am coming."
Psalm 27:8 (NLT)

Be Still
for a
Silent Moment with God

Digging Deeper

In what circumstances do you most often find yourself multi-tasking?

How could you change your focus to concentrate on one thing at a time?

Would this improve your relationships with God and others? How?

Prayer for Today

My life is too busy, God. I feel like I'm juggling so many things; I wish I had three hands! But, seriously, something is missing. Help me to stop living on the surface and dive deeper. I'd love to take this adventure with you. Let's go together. Amen.

Your Thoughts

Walk Humbly

୬

What is God's opinion about the best use of
our time and money? Let's ask him.

Gotta Have It

*I observed that most people are motivated to success
because they envy their neighbors.
But this, too, is meaningless—like chasing the wind.*
Ecclesiastes 4:4 (NLT)

Consider this often-repeated quote: "Too many of us spend
money we don't have on stuff we don't need to impress people
we don't care about." Can you relate?

Our economy thrives on convincing people to buy more
than necessary. We feel deprived if we don't own all the
latest gadgets. If we can't flaunt the hottest new technology,
what will everyone think? Besides, without cool tech, how
would we keep ourselves amused?

But what about our dwindling bank balance and
ballooning debt? Plus, all this buying, selling, and maintaining takes valuable time. Eventually, we may grow weary of

managing all that stuff. A simpler lifestyle and change in perspective may be in order.

Still not convinced? Consider this scenario. Suppose you purchase a motorboat. All your neighbors own one, and you want one too. So you take out a loan, begin monthly payments, buy insurance for it, get a vehicle to tow it, and perhaps rent space to store it. Then you pay for maintenance and put gas in it on top of the other expenses for your two or three trips each summer to the lake. Your new boat consumes tons of time—not to mention thousands in cash!

If you genuinely enjoy boating and go often, such an investment is probably worthwhile. But with limited resources, buying a boat may not be the wisest choice. Maybe a simpler option would be better.

What is God's opinion about the best use of our time and money? Since both ultimately come from him, he might have a different plan. Let's ask him.

If I were still trying to please people,
I would not be a servant of Christ.
Galatians 1:10b (NIV)

Be Still
for a
Silent Moment with God

Digging Deeper

Do you own "stuff" that you don't really need? What kinds of things?

Do those items feed your soul? Or drain your resources? Describe.

How could you seek God's guidance to help you find balance in this area?

Prayer for Today

This is a real struggle for me, God. I have so many possessions that I'm running ragged, trying to keep up with the time and money they demand. Sometimes my belongings seem to own me—not the other way around. Show me what to do. Guide me into a more manageable life. Amen.

Your Thoughts

❧

In the ordinariness of our lives,
we can serve God with excellence.

Super-Hero

He leads the humble in doing right,
teaching them his way.
Psalm 25:9 (NLT)

How do you spend your days? Is your time consumed by routine, boring work? Do you spend hours on a never-ending list of household chores? Do you focus all your energy on caring for others with no moments left for yourself? Do you ever ask yourself, "Is this all there is?"

We long for exciting, important adventures. We would like to be remembered through the ages for some fantastic contribution to civilization. But, really, how reasonable is that? Is this what Jesus intends for us? Perhaps—but probably not.

It's tough to accept that we may serve God best in the humdrum of everyday existence. Realistically, the career path for super-heroes is pretty limited—and that's a good thing. If everyone were a VIP, necessary jobs would go unfilled. Who would do the hard work of making sure our community functions? How would people in need be fed and cared for? Who would keep daily life moving forward?

Most of the world's tasks are accomplished by ordinary folks. As the backbone of society, we keep everything humming along. Millions labor each day to help others, excel at their careers, and set the finest example they can.

Where does that leave you and me? Are our glorious dreams impractical and unattainable? Maybe; maybe not. But regardless, we are critical threads in the fabric holding the world together. It's not always necessary to perform heroic deeds. Our daily efforts are enough.

Jesus asks that we be faithful in the small things. In the ordinariness of our lives, we can serve him with excellence. No matter how simple and humble we may appear, when we stand united, we are an unstoppable force—a tidal wave carrying his message of love.

Let your light shine before others,
that they may see your good deeds
and glorify your Father in heaven.
Matthew 5:16 (NIV)

Be Still
for a
Silent Moment with God

Digging Deeper

Do you have dreams of doing great deeds for God? Describe them.

If he asked you to take a humbler role, how would you adjust?

In what ways could you seek God's guidance for your contribution?

Prayer for Today

I want to do amazing things for you, God! But somehow my path is always blocked. Do you have other ideas for me? Lead me in the way of humility. Show me your plan and how I can serve you as we walk together in the ordinariness of life. Amen.

Your Thoughts

❧

Transform a boring activity
into an encounter with the divine.

Laundry Boycott

Whatever you do, whether in word or deed,
do it all in the name of the Lord Jesus,
giving thanks to God the Father through him.
Colossians 3:17 (NIV)

We have too much to do! Urgent tasks bombard us from all directions. How will we get everything done? Something's got to give.

What makes life so hectic? Even when we sense a clear calling from God, it's hard to devote every ounce of energy to it while juggling all the other balls in our lives. Or we may be mystified about our life's purpose, yet we still stay busy with jobs, family, community, and a host of other obligations.

As we lace up our running shoes to meet all these challenges, we'd rather not be slowed down by trivial, mundane duties. Vital work is at stake! Twenty-four hours just isn't enough time to fit in such important stuff. So we close our eyes and ignore those irritating lesser tasks for as long as possible.

Sometimes I let low priority jobs—like washing clothes—slide to the bottom of my list. Is there a chore you tend to put off, one you really dislike?

We can't boycott the laundry forever, but we can change our perspective. Let's take a lesson from Brother Laurence, who practiced the presence of God in all he did. Even when he was peeling potatoes, he sensed that Jesus was right there with him. He transformed a boring activity into an encounter with the divine.

Jesus is delighted to stay close as we tackle those humdrum chores we've been putting off. With him by our side, even doing the wash can become a sacred experience.

You will show me the way of life,
granting me the joy of your presence
and the pleasures of living with you forever.
Psalm 16:11 (NLT)

༄

Be Still
for a
Silent Moment with God

Digging Deeper

What have you been putting off as you pursue more important tasks?

How could you change your perspective?

If Jesus were there with you, how would that encourage you?

Prayer for Today

I'm overwhelmed, God. There's too much to do and too little time. Serving you is vital, and the small stuff can wait. But that's not really true, is it? Even the tiniest insignificant activity matters when you are with me. Help me to enjoy your presence always and everywhere. Amen.

Your Thoughts

৶

To see all that's possible,
we must expand our vision.

Walk Through the Gate

Wait patiently for the LORD.
Be brave and courageous.
Yes, wait patiently for the LORD.
Psalm 27:14 (NLT)

Many of us know the direction we're going. A cherished dream tugs at our heart—something we hope to do soon. Perhaps we want to serve. Or a creative project beckons our soul. Though our plans may stretch far into the future, our hopes are clear.

Then the unexpected happens. We anticipate new job responsibilities, but a co-worker seems to glide right along the path we hoped to walk. In spite of a stellar record, the opportunity we fervently desire is given to another, and we're left out. We feel overlooked and heartbroken.

What happened? Our passion was strong. We understood that our calling was from God. Now we aren't so sure.

Doubt silently creeps into our souls. Are we moving in the wrong direction? Are we not talented enough? Should we give up on our hopes? Not at all. The most likely answer is that Jesus has something better in mind.

Perhaps it's time to reframe our ambition. Our desires could be too narrow. To see all that's possible, we must expand our vision. We may be seeing only a tiny slice of a vast possibility. Other options are beckoning—countless ways, large and small, to fulfill our dreams. We just need to watch for God's hand pointing to the road that is best.

Look again. Is a special door opening for you—maybe one you have been avoiding? Perhaps the original opportunity wasn't meant for you at all. If God is holding another gate open for you, what are you waiting for? It's time to step through it.

And we know that in all things
God works for the good of those who love him,
who have been called according to his purpose.
Romans 8:28 (NIV)

Be Still
for a
Silent Moment with God

Digging Deeper

What are you doing to make your dreams a reality?

Have you ever felt sidelined in your efforts? Describe the situation.

Could God be leading you to an opportunity you didn't expect? How?

Prayer for Today

My aspirations, the things I want to do in life, mean so much to me. But you, God, know the vast opportunities waiting beyond my vision. Let's walk together through the special gate you have just for me—the one that leads to your best plan. Amen.

Your Thoughts

❧

Are you the sum of your possessions
or a beloved child of God?

Road to Simplicity

One person pretends to be rich, yet has nothing;
another pretends to be poor, yet has great wealth.
Proverbs 13:7 (NIV)

Are you longing for a simpler life—one with fewer complications, noise, and obligations? A calm, restful existence would soothe your frazzled self. But how can you achieve such a goal? Where is God in your struggle?

Material things often distract us from deep spiritual growth. The din of advertising drowns out God's voice. We may wish to focus on Jesus, but we're busy trying to improve our standard of living. What we own and the entertainment we watch define us. The all-pervasive social media doesn't help either. Perhaps it's time to begin letting go.

Try this mental exercise. Picture yourself walking in search of a scaled-back lifestyle. You pass blocks of shops screaming for you to buy. Noisy intersections are filled with brand-new cars. Everywhere are advertisements about the latest tech. You're tempted, but you continue on. At the end, you find your sanctuary. A peaceful meadow and a quiet stream await you, just perfect for relaxation and reflection.

Emerging from a culture of greed and superficiality is challenging. But consider whether you are merely the sum of your possessions or a beloved child of God. Does your happiness depend on gathering more and more stuff? Or is it time to set your burden down, knowing you have nothing left to prove or gain?

Down through the ages, Christians have put aside wealth to fix their attention on God. This may be your path too. Do you see Jesus waiting at the bend in the road? Will you join him? You belong to Christ forever. That really is enough.

Keep your lives free from the love of money
and be content with what you have, because God has said,
"Never will I leave you; never will I forsake you."
Hebrews 13:5 (NIV)

Be Still
for a
Silent Moment with God

Digging Deeper

What are your simplicity challenges?

How do they interfere with your spiritual growth?

What changes do you sense God is asking of you?

Prayer for Today

It's so easy to get caught up in today's consumer culture. Everywhere I go, messages entice me with the benefits of buying product after product. But I know most of it isn't what you want for me, God. Show me what I really need. Walk with me as I scale back to make more room for you. Amen.

Your Thoughts

❧

Keep moving ahead
in the direction that you're called.

A Tiny Speck

*For God is working in you,
giving you the desire and the power
to do what pleases him.*
Philippians 2:13 (NLT)

It's easy to feel overwhelmed. So much is going on, so many tasks to do. But we have too many moving parts, too many pieces in play. Getting it all done is impossible.

We try our best to meet every demand, but we aren't perfect multi-taskers. Soon we slip further and further behind our own expectations. Feelings of inadequacy bubble to the surface. If we were better parents, spouses, employees, or you name it, everything would somehow fall into place.

Our friends and family seem to do fine. Media celebrities radiate confidence and success. But how do they do it? And what's wrong with us?

Actually, nothing. Remember, we can't peer into their souls. They live in this society, too, and undoubtedly face obstacles similar to our own. We aren't alone.

But then there's our Christian world. We may struggle in our own devotional time or with a ministry project. We long for deep intimacy and wonderful outcomes. But when our efforts yield little result, nothing seems worthwhile. We begin to doubt our calling. Jesus invited us into this spiritual life. Surely he could make it a bit easier, couldn't he?

Before you get overwhelmed again, stop and consider a fresh perspective. In God's universe, we are only little specks with a tiny piece of the action. Even the most productive among us can't really boast monumental accomplishments. But in our own way, each of us moves the needle of progress through every small step. Who we are can still make a difference.

You don't have to perform heroic deeds. Every detail need not be perfect. Just keep moving ahead in the direction that you're called. God will do the rest.

> *Let's not get tired of doing what is good.*
> *At just the right time*
> *we will reap a harvest of blessing*
> *if we don't give up.*
> *Galatians 6:9 (NLT)*

Be Still
for a
Silent Moment with God

Digging Deeper

Describe your greatest frustration.

Can you see any progress, however small?

How do you sense God is working with you in this area?

Prayer for Today

Sometimes I feel so discouraged. I'm trying—really, I am—but the pace is slow. I believe you've called me to important work, God, but there are so many roadblocks. Lift me onto your shoulder. Hold me tight as I learn how, in my little corner of your universe, my efforts matter. Amen.

Your Thoughts

When we clear away the clutter,
it's much easier to see God.

Buying Dishes

Why spend money on what is not bread,
and your labor on what does not satisfy?
Isaiah 55:2a (NIV)

In our consumer culture, simplicity is a challenging virtue. It often feels odd, conflicting, and just plain weird. Why lead a simple, modest life if the world offers us luxuries? What's the benefit of a quiet, uncomplicated life when there are so many fun diversions?

Lately I've been pondering dishes. We have an attractive white set for every day. There's nothing wrong with it; each piece still looks nice. We also inherited my grandmother's antique china. But such finery doesn't fit our lifestyle, so we intend to sell them. It's all part of my empty-nester downsizing plan.

But occasionally, an extra plate or two comes in handy when we entertain guests. So I scoured the ads and found a cute set that was vastly marked down. It seemed a terrific deal, and I was pleased with my shopping ability—until I realized it had 24 bowls and lots of other pieces we would never use. That's way too much clutter for no reason.

So I canceled the order and bought four plates in our original pattern instead. Problem solved—but I grieved, knowing I wouldn't be unwrapping cool new stuff. Having lived a modest lifestyle for years, I was surprised by my disappointment.

Discovering and buying fun new things can entice us away from the simple life. Whether it's the lure of the chase or keeping up with neighbors, piling up possessions we don't need can be a trap.

A simpler lifestyle may be a tough choice, but a necessary one. When we clear away the clutter, it's much easier to see God.

For where your treasure is,
there your heart will be also.
Luke 12:34 (NIV)

Be Still
for a
Silent Moment with God

Digging Deeper

Is simplicity a difficult choice for you? In what ways?

If you'd like to scale back your lifestyle, how could you do it?

How might you partner with God to achieve your goal?

Prayer for Today

I love to snag a good deal, God, even if I don't really need it. Opening a new package is such a thrill. But extra stuff just complicates my world. Help me see the way of life you have for me. Walk with me as I learn to live in simplicity. Amen.

Your Thoughts

ès

Everyone longs to be
understood and respected.

Blah Blah Blah

Set a guard over my mouth, LORD;
keep watch over the door of my lips.
Psalm 141:3 (NIV)

Three old friends sip lattes at the coffee shop. Their conversation is lively and peppered with stories and opinions. But are they listening to each other? Judging by their body language, perhaps not. Odd as it may seem, it's not hard to imagine them as three sets of teeth—chattering on, separate and alone.

Similar conversations take place in our lives every day. Sometimes our minds are made up, and we simply don't care about other views. Perhaps we already know what our companions will say, so why listen? Or we could be busy concentrating on our next point, so we can prove our brilliance.

But interactions like this don't strengthen relationships. Instead, they separate us. Everyone longs to be understood and respected. Others often seek our attention and acceptance. When friends and loved ones share thoughts and feel valued, we build connections.

Humble listeners are rare jewels. They may not speak often, but when they do, ears perk up. Their few words carry weight. Their expressions are infrequent, yet well thought out. Many want to hear what they have to say.

In conversation, we gingerly extend our hand, offering a belief or vision. Will we be honored? Even if no one agrees, we hope they consider our ideas with respect. When people listen and respond with their whole selves—not just a chattering set of teeth—we feel valued.

Each of us is special, and yet Jesus works in everyone. Listening carefully not only honors God and the other person, but it might even change our perspective. We still may not agree, but showing reverence by truly hearing others can deepen our own Christian life.

To answer before listening—
that is folly and shame.
Proverbs 18:13 (NIV)

Be Still
for a
Silent Moment with God

Digging Deeper

Do you do most of the talking in your conversations?

How might you engage with folks differently, so they feel valued?

Is God leading you to make some changes in how you relate to others? In what ways?

Prayer for Today

Sometimes I'm so eager to share my thoughts, I jump in and dominate the conversation. But this is hurtful to my friends and family. Help me, God. Hold me back and show me how to take time to listen—really listen. I don't have all the brilliant ideas. There is much I can learn from hearing others. Amen.

Your Thoughts

ॐ

Practice your faith daily,
and you'll make an impression on others.

Not Forgotten

Your faithfulness continues through all generations;
you established the earth, and it endures.
Psalm 119:90 (NIV)

What is most important to you? Is it your faith? Your unique way of seeing the world? Or maybe your favorite music, art, or literature? This is your truth. This is what matters to you, and you want it to continue—hopefully, for years after you're gone.

Leaving a lasting legacy can be tricky. One way to be remembered is by personal achievements. You might write a book, record a song, or become a community or faith leader. Any of these avenues could give recognition to your ideas and values.

The drawback is that these efforts entail a lot of work, plus they may require some special talent. Then you'd need to generate some level of fame, or nobody will notice you. Even so, the attention of the public is fleeting. You might soon be forgotten. Unfortunately, your passions and convictions would likely be laid to rest with you.

Why not try just living your truth every day? That's the humbler, easier, and perhaps more effective route. Practice your faith daily, and you'll inevitably make an impression on others. Support the arts so that they continue to be alive and vibrant for a new generation. Take part in public conversations, and let your viewpoint influence the community. Your life example can subtly shape the future.

As Christians, we stand in a long stream with believers who have walked before us. Their faithful contributions, however insignificant, swirl together in the cool waters we now enjoy. How do we impart these values? Our contribution doesn't require heroic action so much as merely continuing in the flow. The essence of our lives and faithfulness can build a foundation for those yet to come.

Let love and faithfulness never leave you;
bind them around your neck,
write them on the tablet of your heart.
Proverbs 3:3 (NIV)

Be Still
for a
Silent Moment with God

Digging Deeper

What matters to you? Describe your deepest values.

How could you live in such a way that others would carry on your interests?

In what ways do you feel Jesus is leading you in this area?

Prayer for Today

My contribution is small, God, and yet it's important. Help me shape a more just, faithful, and beautiful creation. I long to live faithfully and leave a world that is more lovely and fair for all. Be with me and guide me as we pursue this dream together. Amen.

Your Thoughts

&

Isn't feeding our souls more important
than filling our shopping bags?

Bling

The LORD doesn't see things the way you see them.
People judge by outward appearance,
but the LORD looks at the heart.
1 Samuel 16:7b (NLT)

A video clip featured pre-teen girls shopping for all the latest "stuff." One young lady said that if she didn't buy her clothes from the best stores, ugly rumors would spread at school, and this would be bad. Are our daughters on a dangerous path? Are we?

Beautiful women have been admired for ages. But lately, we've reached new extremes. Airbrushed supermodels flood our computer screens. Magazines feature movie stars with flawless makeup and hair. Social media demands perfection. When we fall short, as everyone does, we feel inadequate. Somehow, we just don't quite measure up.

If we, as schoolgirls, were taught that our highest value was in the bling we buy, own, and wear, how does that affect our lives today? Do we see ourselves as valuable people with much to offer, professionally and personally? I hope we do. But for many, valuing ourselves can be challenging—especially if we are affirmed mainly for our appearance.

And what about our souls? At some point, we may endure an emptiness that possessions just can't fill. As we leave the bling behind, we yearn to know that we're enough. We want God to love us for who we are. Sadly, we and many of today's young women are set up by society for major spiritual struggles down the road.

Isn't feeding our souls more important than filling our shopping bags? There's no need to spiff ourselves up for God. We have infinite worth in his eyes. He treasures us just as we are. No bling required!

> *You are altogether beautiful, my darling;*
> *there is no flaw in you.*
> *Song of Songs 4:7 (NIV)*

Be Still
for a
Silent Moment with God

Digging Deeper

Are you easily influenced by ads promising that products, like a new shade of lipstick, will solve your problems? Describe.

How could you change your perspective?

What do you think God is telling you about your worth?

Prayer for Today

I've heard it for so long, I hardly notice anymore. "Buy this outfit, and you'll look beautiful. Use this shampoo and see your troubles disappear." Help me overcome these temptations, God. Show me that I'm lovely in your sight, just the way I am—no bling necessary. Amen.

Your Thoughts

With Your God

❧

Slow down and keep
the main thing the main thing.

Tricks of the Trade

The LORD is near to all who call on him,
to all who call on him in truth.
Psalm 145:18 (NIV)

Let's hear it for fortune cookies! Who hasn't gleaned at least
a kernel of wisdom from these sweet little gems? Recently,
my husband and I visited our favorite Chinese restaurant.
My fortune said, "If you're too busy learning the tricks of
the trade, you may never learn the trade."

Fortune cookie writers crank out predictions every day
from their workshops across the sea. Do they know they're
handing out spiritual advice? Probably not, but they are.

Many of us work hard on our Christian life. We go to
church, do Bible study, and attend prayer meetings. Don't
forget teaching Sunday school, organizing the congregational
picnic, and singing in the choir. Whew!

As we perfect these tools of our spiritual lives, we often overlook the key reason for our devotion—Jesus. He's standing on our front porch, hoping we'll let him in. Will we open the door? Or are we occupied elsewhere, leaving an empty house with a doorbell that nobody answers?

Let's adjust our focus and concentrate on our trade, rather than the tools. Even a slight shift provides an opportunity to nurture our relationship with God. Instead of trying to fit in more activities, consider passing a few on to someone else. Keep only the ones that tug at your heartstrings and leave more time for Jesus.

It's easy to get caught up in all our religious pursuits. Letting go of a few can free up sacred, undisturbed moments to be with Jesus. Slow down and keep the main thing the main thing.

Jesus replied, "All who love me will do what I say.
My Father will love them,
and we will come and
make our home with each of them."
John 14:23 (NLT)

Be Still
for a
Silent Moment with God

Digging Deeper

Does your busy life leave scarcely any space for God? Describe how that happens.

In what ways is he calling you to spend more time with him?

How could you free up your schedule?

Prayer for Today

I mean well, God. I honestly do. Serving you is important, so I keep taking on more responsibilities. After all, the church needs me. But I know you want me more. Help me cut through the jungle of commitments. Give me time to enjoy with you. Amen.

Your Thoughts

༄

It can be tough to listen
and act on God's message.

By Ear

Don't just listen to God's word.
You must do what it says.
Otherwise, you are only fooling yourselves.
James 1:22 (NLT)

I once heard a story about a Christian who died and went to Heaven. The immense beauty was dazzling. But then he walked into a strange room with piles of human ears reaching to the ceiling. His guide explained, "These ears belonged to those who listened to the word of God on Sundays, but did nothing about it."

What a creepy story! And yet it holds a nugget of truth. This tale isn't really about ears, but our lives. Are we called to listen for God's special message to each of us and to act on it?

For many of us, the world seems happy and fulfilling enough. But sometimes we sense a void. A vague feeling nags our souls. Could we be on the wrong track? Is Jesus nudging us toward a new path, asking that we take a stand or serve others? If we ignore these thoughts, will they fade away? We may know what's right, but just don't get around to responding.

On the other hand, something within might be seriously amiss. Perhaps we struggle with a crippling personal difficulty, like an addiction. Deep down, we realize there's a problem. But whenever troubles bubble up, we shove them back below the surface. When we hear God's voice, we would rather look the other way than deal with the issue.

It can be tough to listen and act on God's message. Even a slight change of direction is a challenge. Committing to tackle our issues may be one of the hardest things we'll ever do. But who wants to end up in a stack of dead ears? Jesus doesn't want that, and neither do we.

> *Jesus replied, "But even more blessed are all*
> *who hear the word of God*
> *and put it into practice."*
> *Luke 11:28 (NLT)*

Be Still
for a
Silent Moment with God

Digging Deeper

Do you sense God urging you to do something different? What needs to change?

How can you tell if Jesus is really speaking to you?

Describe a small step you could take to shift your direction.

Prayer for Today

I know you're calling me to change and grow, God, but it feels scary. Often I push those thoughts away, but that's not a good idea. Help me to listen and do what you ask. Your hand will guide me through every challenge. Together we can do it. Amen.

Your Thoughts

୬

A breathing space offers time
to refocus on what truly matters.

Pushing Pause

In repentance and rest is your salvation,
in quietness and trust is your strength.
Isaiah 30:15b (NIV)

Hard-driving people are everywhere. That's how I am, and you may be too. We're always on the go, pushing toward the next goal or achievement. Our world never stops, even for a moment. But a brief article by John Ruskin changed my perspective.

Ruskin writes that life is like a song. Our voices enthusiastically join the chorus. But as we harmonize each note, suddenly a rest appears on the page. We're forced to be quiet until our theme shows up again. But who wants to just sit around? We need our continuous melody.

For those who don't read music, here is a quick explanation. The dots on the score are notes to play. Special marks called rests direct us when to be silent.

Ruskin cautions against leaving out the rests. We may think there is no melody in silence, but each pause actually carries the echo of music within it. Continuous notes, played without even the slightest breathing space, become noise. Quiet times shape our life song and give a much-needed respite.

This may sound like bad news for our hard-charging selves. We often see little benefit in stopping to rest. We're made for glorious achievements, and we must move ahead to realize our potential. But there is value in a pause. Quietly observing a flower or hummingbird opens our souls to God's beauty. More importantly, a breathing space offers time to refocus on what truly matters.

Is it challenging for you to stop and rest? What if you miss something or get stuck? Try it and you'll find that, despite the pauses of life, our songs continue. Even when the tune seems faint and far away, we can still hum along with God.

> *Truly my soul finds rest in God;*
> *my salvation comes from him.*
> *Psalm 62:1a (NIV)*

Be Still
for a
Silent Moment with God

Digging Deeper

Do you find breathing space important, or is it a waste of time? Why?

How can you add restful moments to your day?

What might you learn about God as you push the pause button?

Prayer for Today

Life is just so busy, God. I'll never get where I'm going if I don't move ahead at full speed. But am I missing something? If I stop and linger, I may see you reflected in a flower, a bird, or a pool of water. Join me as we hear music in the silence of your creation. Amen.

Your Thoughts

৯৯

As we unwind and refresh,
new perspectives appear.

Hidden Jewels

I wait for the LORD, my whole being waits,
and in his word I put my hope.
Psalm 130:5 (NIV)

Are you a hidden jewel? You have a lot to offer, yet you're held back in obscurity. Nobody else seems to notice you. Even when you bring it up with God, he asks you to stay put for a while.

It's tough and frustrating. Many of us yearn to be out front. We long to be recognized. We want our lives to count, to make an impact, to change the world. Whatever our dreams, we believe they should come true—right this minute.

But sometimes Jesus holds up his hand and says, "No, not now." It seems like a hard answer, but maybe we are hidden for a reason. He may have a secret mission just for us. What feels like stagnation could actually be building us up spiritually for his next move.

What happens while we wait? How can we keep our aspirations in check without feeling demoralized? Rather than kick against the giant stop sign, a better strategy might be to accept it.

This is an opportunity for rest. God provides a sanctuary—a special garden space where we can grow as we linger. During this interval, take time to relax, stretch out, and breathe. As we unwind and refresh ourselves, new perspectives and opportunities begin to appear.

As we soak up the sun and bathe in life-giving streams, it's important to listen for God's voice, encouraging our growth. At just the right moment, we'll be visible again, like jewels sparkling in the sunlight. Jesus appears in the distance, beckoning us to step forward. Our time has come to roll past the stop sign.

This vision is for a future time.
It describes the end, and it will be fulfilled.
If it seems slow in coming, wait patiently,
for it will surely take place. It will not be delayed.
Habakkuk 2:3 (NLT)

Be Still
for a
Silent Moment with God

Digging Deeper

Does it seem like your life isn't moving forward? Describe how you feel stuck.

How might you accept this season and continue growing?

How do you see God's work in this situation?

Prayer for Today

Sometimes I'm so frustrated, God. I know I could do wonderful things for you. But barriers—tons of them—block my way. Help me cherish this time of hiddenness and growth. When the right time comes, we'll walk together into the sunlight, hand-in-hand. Amen.

Your Thoughts

❧

Great risk requires great faith,
but we are never alone.

Taking a Risk

This is my command—be strong and courageous!
Do not be afraid or discouraged.
For the LORD your God is with you wherever you go.
Joshua 1:9 (NLT)

Risk-taking sounds adventurous. Risk-taking sounds brave. Risk-taking sounds glamorous. But it can also be downright scary!

It's fun to think of ourselves as risk-takers. But we aren't really taking a risk unless we stand to suffer—perhaps a lot. Exciting rewards are tempting, but the possibility of significant pain or loss must balance our hopes. Risk carries both outcomes.

Before taking a risk, it's important to consider how much we're willing to lose. Perhaps we don't want to give up what we already have. We may fear alienating those close to us who might be affected. Maybe we could tolerate a few minor risks, limit the damage, but still appear bold to everyone else.

Are we being honest with ourselves? We'd like to think we're fearless and willing to step out in courage. But inside, we may just desire to be comfy and content. We are glad to take a risk as long as there isn't too big a negative impact. But often it's simpler to choose the easier road to a more secure future.

Suppose we sense God calling us to a venture for which we are not prepared or have even considered. Do we continue to follow him through uncertainty and turbulent times? Do we willingly make the sacrifices he asks for, trusting that all will be okay? Pursuing a dream he has placed in our hearts is challenging. But the rewards and growth are worth the risk, even when we fall short of our goal.

Great risk requires great faith, but we are never alone. Jesus is faithful, and he will see us through. Look—he's up ahead, inviting you and me to a grand adventure.

> *Jesus looked at them intently and said,*
> *"Humanly speaking, it is impossible.*
> *But with God everything is possible."*
> *Matthew 19:26 (NLT)*

Be Still
for a
Silent Moment with God

Digging Deeper

Do you yearn to step out and take a bold action? Describe your dream.

What is stopping you?

Where do you see God in your grand adventure?

Prayer for Today

I like to think of myself as brave and courageous. But maybe that isn't true. My greatest dreams also involve great costs. Am I willing to bear them? Help me, God. Hold my hand and reassure me. You've called me to act, and I know you won't forsake me. Amen.

Your Thoughts

ക

Each new season adds
a special harmony to our lives.

God's Orchestra

For everything there is a season,
a time for every activity under heaven.
Ecclesiastes 3:1 (NLT)

Have you ever attended an orchestra concert? If you sit up close, you can see the interplay of the instruments. Perhaps the violins catch the melody first, and then the flutes run with it. The drums pound the beat as the trumpets join in at the end. Even the lowly triangle has its moment of glory. Yet each performs under the watchful eye and baton of the conductor.

Our lives hold a striking similarity. Some friends are with us forever. Others appear only for a season. Some of us remain in one beloved home for years. Others are always on the move. Sometimes these life changes feel good. Other times, we sense a twinge of sadness when important people and places are lost.

Our personal melody is similar. We may pursue a career and keep it for a lifetime. Or we might jump between professions, bringing our unique talents to each one. No matter how impressive or humble our tune, it's part of God's masterpiece.

The seasons of our years shift too. Dreams and goals of our youth give way to a calm and inviting presence as we age. The desires of our hearts change as we gain fresh perspective. Each new season adds a special harmony to our lives.

We are all members of God's orchestra. He weaves companionship and opportunities into our world. Then sometimes he ties off a thread and begins another one. The melodies change. Some are boisterous. Some are scarcely above a whisper. Through it all, God brings forth a beautiful sound.

"For I know the plans I have for you,"
declares the LORD,
"plans to prosper you and not to harm you,
plans to give you hope and a future."
Jeremiah 29:11 (NIV)

Be Still
for a
Silent Moment with God

Digging Deeper

What's going on in your section of God's orchestra?

How do beginnings and endings in the music affect you?

When do you hear God weaving your tune into his symphony?

Prayer for Today

I'm totally jazzed, God, to be a vital instrument in your orchestra. It's hard for me, though, when treasured friends leave or exciting opportunities end. Comfort me and help me remember that my tiny melody is part of your grand design. Let's make beautiful music together. Amen.

Your Thoughts

❦
Why not do what's possible today?
God will lead the way.

Opportunity Knocks

Commit to the LORD whatever you do,
and he will establish your plans.
The LORD works out everything to its proper end.
Proverbs 16:3-4a (NIV)

Have you ever put your life on hold, waiting for the perfect opportunity to appear? Or maybe you're working on a project and feel stalled, uncertain about which way to go. For many of us, this is a familiar story. Nobody wants to move in the wrong direction or risk straying outside of God's plan.

Opportunities, both large and small, often dangle before our eyes—but we don't always see them. Perhaps we're blinded by our desire for a plum assignment that perfectly matches our dream job. The gig must also promise success and be easy to accomplish with little effort and no overtime.

Or have you ever been stuck on a task and needed a solution? A thunderbolt from heaven, showing the way, would be nice in those situations. Even a gentle nudge would help.

But God doesn't always offer a clear road map with everything outlined in painstaking detail. Instead, he asks us to trust and move ahead, knowing the next steps will be revealed.

A ministry leader I know, when confronted with uncertainty, used to say, "Try something. It might work." There is much wisdom in this simple advice. Rather than agonize over a decision, why not look at the options, pick one, and try it? If it works, that's great. If it doesn't, don't despair. Just make a different choice.

We all have opportunities right in front of us. Don't wait for the best time or the perfect circumstance. Why not do what's possible today? God will lead the way. Let's get moving!

I know all the things you do,
and I have opened a door for you
that no one can close.
Revelation 3:8a (NLT)

Be Still
for a
Silent Moment with God

Digging Deeper

Have you put dreams on hold? What are they?

What are your choices—even ones that may be disguised as bad ideas?

How could you trust God to show you the way as you step out in faith?

Prayer for Today

Sometimes I feel at loose ends, God. When I'm confused about which way to go, I don't go anywhere. But that's not what you want for me. Help me move ahead and pursue the good opportunities in front of me right now. Guide me as we walk down your path together. Amen.

Your Thoughts

❧

The meantime always has room for
growth and service, laughter and tears.

In the Meantime

The LORD says, "I will guide you along
the best pathway for your life.
I will advise you and watch over you."
Psalm 32:8 (NLT)

"What will we do in the meantime?" This is a common question when we find ourselves between two life events. Perhaps we recently graduated and look forward to our wedding. Or maybe we're newly retired and wonder how to fill our golden years until we greet Jesus face-to-face.

The time between great milestones is important. Smaller intervals shape our lives too. The minutes between sunrise and sundown are significant. So is the space between one weekend and the next. Whether these interludes are days, months, or longer, time matters.

What are we doing during these in-between moments? For me, I often feel like I'm just treading water. It's easy to be unfocused when we're between time-markers. There doesn't seem to be much to do except watch the days slowly fade out of sight. Can we find a better way?

The meantime can be a stage of transition as we pivot into an unfamiliar direction. Jesus may ask us to prepare for fresh responsibilities. Or a new relationship might beckon. Sadly, this could also be a season of mourning. Either way, it's not a passive period. God always offers a chance to partake fully in life.

Is the meantime different from other times? Not really. Sometimes God calls us to wait on his timing, and that's good. But even if we pause for a bit, I doubt he wants everything to come to a screeching halt. The meantime always has room for growth and service, laughter and tears.

Your own ears will hear him.
Right behind you a voice will say,
"This is the way you should go,"
whether to the right or to the left.
Isaiah 30:21 (NLT)

Be Still
for a
Silent Moment with God

Digging Deeper

Have you struggled with being "in between?" Describe one such moment in your life.

How could you reframe any inertia you feel during those seasons?

In what ways do you sense God's hand leading you forward?

Prayer for Today

Sometimes being "in the meantime" is confusing, God. I may be between milestones in my life. Or a new direction might loom just ahead, but I can't see it yet. Either way, I need you! As we walk together through this interim time, guide me on the best path to follow. Amen.

Your Thoughts

᷍

Jesus is offering his soothing hand.
Why not simply trust him?

Taming the Worry Monster

Give all your worries and cares to God,
for he cares about you.
1 Peter 5:7 (NLT)

Air turbulence on flights is scary! At least, that's my opinion. You may be one of those fearless travelers who blithely carry on like nothing is happening, but not me. When the airplane begins to shake, I grab both armrests and hold on tight. Then I pray and worry until I'm back on land again. (But mostly I just worry.)

A recent trip offered a startling revelation. I've always been somehow convinced that if I worry enough, the plane will stay in the air. How crazy is that? I know God, not me, is the one who keeps the universe going. So why would I think my fear could keep an airplane aloft at 30,000 feet? Silly me.

So, this time I made a conscious decision to turn the plane's fate over to the person with the power—Jesus.

Suddenly my anxiety lifted, and I let go of the armrests. Even with the turbulence, I felt peaceful and calm. It was a pleasant flight, and I wasn't exhausted when the plane landed.

How many times have we done this in other areas of our lives? Although we know better, something in us fervently believes worrying helps—that if we fret enough, everything will be just fine. But if we slack off in the worry department, tragedy awaits and our world crumbles—at least we think so.

We are not as powerful as we assume. While being reasonably careful is important, we're not in control. As Scripture tells us, worry can't add a single moment to our lifespan. Only God can do that.

So why not simply trust Jesus? He's offering his soothing hand. If we hold on tight, he'll silence the worry monster in each of us.

Don't worry about anything;
instead, pray about everything.
Tell God what you need
and thank him for all he has done.
Philippians 4:6 (NLT)

Be Still
for a
Silent Moment with God

Digging Deeper

Have you ever been saved from disaster by worrying? Explain the situation.

What are a few ways you could trust more and worry less?

Where does God figure into your concerns?

Prayer for Today

I'm a chronic worrier, God, but you already know that. I am convinced that if I just fulfill my quota of worrying, everything will be fine. But I missed something. The universe is always under your control. Help me relax and breathe. All is well. Amen.

Your Thoughts

≫

Relax—Jesus has it covered.
You're safe with him.

The Tie That Binds

This I declare about the LORD:
He alone is my refuge, my place of safety;
he is my God, and I trust him.
Psalm 91:2 (NLT)

About a hundred years ago, several men were preparing a dirigible for flight. Although we seldom find such aircraft these days, they are like blimps that just float up and away.

The dirigible had ropes all around with a man holding each one, keeping the ship on the ground until time to launch. But a powerful wind suddenly blew in and lifted the airship. It began to fly higher and higher. Most of the men immediately dropped their ropes, but one person remained unaccounted for.

When the group finally found the dirigible after its flight, the missing man was still with the ship. "What happened?"

his friends asked. "How did you hold on so long? We're amazed you survived."

The man replied, "I didn't hold on. God held me." After the wind gust lifted him up, he tied the rope around his waist. That way, he wasn't forced to rely on his grip. God and the rope kept him aloft and set him down safely.

Still, the man's friends seemed perplexed. If he was holding the rope, how could he also tie it? Simple—he had been trained in the military to tie a one-handed knot. Not only did Jesus save him in flight; he prepared him first.

God's love and protection are apparent throughout this tale. We often believe we succeed in life through our own efforts. Rarely, we stop to remember that God's rope is what protects and enables us to carry out his special plans. So relax. Jesus has it covered. Just keep his rope securely around your waist. You're safe with him.

You will keep in perfect peace
all who trust in you,
all whose thoughts are fixed on you!
Isaiah 26:3 (NLT)

Be Still
for a
Silent Moment with God

Digging Deeper

Do you sometimes believe everything is up to you? Describe how that pressure feels.

In what ways do you perceive God keeping you safe?

How could you begin to let go and trust God's rope?

Prayer for Today

I have such a hard time trusting. I know you're there, God, and I can count on you. But I continually fall back into my old independent life. Tie your rope around my waist and keep me from all harm. You and I will be together, today and always. Amen.

Your Thoughts

The Journey Continues

The Micah way of life—to act justly, love mercy, and walk humbly with God—is a challenge. The real world doesn't always value these traits. We may seem out of step with close friends and family, not to mention the rest of society. We may not fit in. Being different can feel uncomfortable, to say the least.

To those around us, we may appear countercultural or even radical. It's hard for them to understand the choices we make between what the world teaches and what we believe is right. We're in excellent company, though. Christians through the ages have also been called radicals as they lived out their ideals of justice, mercy, and humility. Yet their stories continue to inspire, even today.

Where are you on the journey? Are you dipping your toe tentatively into the stream of change? Or are you already living an authentic Micah life? Like most of us, you're probably somewhere in between. Wherever you are in the process, that's great. God loves you and is delighted with you.

Each day brings fresh opportunities. Whatever we face, let's be gentle with ourselves. It's easy to become overwhelmed or discouraged. Occasionally we just need to stop for a cup of cool water and some rest.

No matter where we are on the trek, our journey continues. Sometimes we move forward with confidence. Other times our progress seems halting and uncertain. We accept that our lives will never be perfect, yet we press ahead. With Jesus by our side, we're on an exciting expedition.

Let's bask in these comforting words from Scripture as we consider our next steps on the Micah way.

> *The LORD keeps you from all harm*
> *and watches over your life.*
> *The LORD keeps watch over you as you come and go,*
> *both now and forever.*
> *Psalm 121:7-8 (NLT)*

As our moments together draw to a close, let's join in a prayer of thanksgiving and hope for the future.

Thank you so much, God, for this time with you. Our travels have taken us from the land of justice, to the fields of mercy, to the flowing streams of humility. You've offered encouragement, guidance, and love throughout our journey. Be our companion as we walk the Micah road, both today and forevermore. Amen.

May the peace of the Lord be always with you.

Lisa

About the Author

Lisa Aré Wulf is an award-winning women's devotional author. Her print, audio, and e-books have been finalists in the USA Best Book Awards, Next Generation Indie Book Awards, and Voice Arts Awards. Publications across the country have featured Lisa's articles on Christian living and spiritual growth. She is a recognized speaker who shares her faith journey with transparency and authority.

A graduate of Fuller Theological Seminary, Lisa also holds two degrees from the University of Colorado. She is an adjunct accounting professor, owned a CPA firm, served in elected public office, and was a professional orchestral musician.

Lisa lives in Colorado with her husband, Calvin, and enjoys the beautiful mountain scenery. They have four children and are happy empty nesters.

For more information about Lisa Aré Wulf, please visit LisaAreWulf.com.